A Story About Stories

# Alex Pickens III

Tending Vision

Michigan

Copyright

Copyright © 2023 by Alex Pickens III. All rights reserved.

Published by Tending Vision, LLC, Okemos, MI.

No part of this publication may be reproduced, stored in a retrieval system, or transmitted in any form or by any means, electronic, mechanical, photocopying, recording, scanning or otherwise, except as permitted under Section 107 or 108 of the 1976 United States Copyright Act, without either the prior permission of the Publisher.

Limit of Liability / Disclaimer of Warranty: While the publisher and author have used their best efforts in preparing this book, they make no representations or warranties with respect to the accuracy or completeness of the contents of this book and specifically disclaim any implied warranties of merchantability or fitness for a particular purpose. No warranty may be created or extended by sales representatives or written sales materials. The advice and strategies contained herein may not be suitable for your situation. You should consult with a professional where appropriate. Neither the publisher nor the author shall be liable for damages arising therefrom.

ISBN: 9798860424197

Dedication

To Naudia

You are my reward for all earthly toil.

Table of Contents

Copyright..............................................2
Dedication ...........................................4
Table of Contents...............................5
Preface................................................7
Introduction: .....................................10
Chapter 1: A Drive To The Lake ......16
Chapter 2: Uninformed Optimism ....25
Chapter 3: Informed Pessimism.......34
Chapter 4: Sensing Valley of Despair ......................................................45
Chapter 5: Entering Valley of Despair ......................................................53
Chapter 6: Through the Valley of Despair..............................................62
Chapter 7: Informed Optimism.........75
Chapter 8: Success...........................82
Fruit of Spirit......................................85
Love: A Downstairs Neighbor ..........85
Joy: Story Time .................................90

Peace: A Simple Question ...............96
Patience: Ride Along Reflections...101
Kindness: A Brick, A Knife ............106
Goodness: A Promise & A Prayer..112
Gentleness: Light Duty...................115
Faithfulness: A Voice In The Wilderness ......................................123
Self-Control: Go and Knock ..........129
One For The Road: A Happy Ending ....................................................138
Addendum......................................145
Acknowledgements........................148
Bibliography ..................................155
About The Author...........................159

Preface

Dreams teach because we're still.

Graduation includes pomp, circumstance, and a silly hat. Hiking a gown, I climbed the stairs. One handshake, then another, before a degree presentation and photo pause. Smile; pump fist; exit. Descending the steps, I saw her to my right.

My mother, six years in a grave, summoned me out of the graduation procession. "Congratulations, Alex. It's time to put it all together now." I hugged her neck and whispered, "I miss you, girl." Her last words were, "All together now." Entreaties to stay and tightening of grip left me whispering to a tear-stained pillow.

The pillow has since been washed, but the pillow-talker is still whispering.

I still whisper, "I miss you girl." A dream is the only place I could get away with calling my mother a girl. Patricia McCallum Pickens, a Southern educator, demanded handles on names: Mr., Mrs., Miss, Ms., Dr., or Rev. Our relationship left no room for chumminess, but graves change things.

Dreams change things.

Dreams teach because we are still. From the grave, my school-teaching mother reminded me to put it *All Together Now*.

Putting it all together means gathering snowflakes of experience and making something meaningful: a snowball, a snowman, or a snow castle. I heard her require that my strands of existential disconnect be woven into a hat, scarf, or afghan. Meaning and insignificance; love and hate; hope and hurt; thirst and contentment are dangling threads. This book is my public response to her private command.

I will put it all together by juxtaposing the pain and promise, observed among first responders, to the heartbreaking yet life-giving story of Elijah the Tishbite. An Old Testament prophet, Elijah experienced what Brian Moran, author of *The 12-Week Year,* calls the emotional cycle of change[i]. My mother's death has taken me through the emotional cycle. Change in your life puts the cycle in your muscles and members.

Members of the Tending Vision blogging community have coaxed the publication of private ruminations. What is more private than a dream or more public than a book? My mother appeared in a dream, and you are holding the result.

Karl Barth[ii], a world-renowned theologian, was asked to summarize his life's work in one sentence. Barth quipped, "Jesus loves me, this I know, for my mother told me so."

My mother told me to put it all together, and that's what I'm going to do.

Introduction:

Weaving a braid was a cub scout requirement. I sat on the kitchen floor while my parents arranged the ropes. They are unseen in my recollection; standing behind me and looking down, over my shoulder. We were focused on three strands, knotted at one end. The other ends of rope were left dangling; a table leg was between me and the knot. I was anxious because I needed the badge to get my next patch[iii]. Both of my parents helped, but I remember my mother leading the braiding exercise.

Maybe she was excited because she gave birth to boys and missed the opportunity to regularly braid a head of hair. Maybe her own scouting days intensified a desire. Whatever the motivation, even forty years later, I can remember their zeal. They wanted me to learn the lesson, but they also had skin in the game. Their pasts or their passions raised the stakes much higher than my badge. What was important to me was not the most important thing.

What is important to us is not the most important thing. My parents' reasons for helping surpassed my reasons for seeking help. A well of experience, deeper than my scouting, sat deeply within them both. Perhaps remembering my conception, birth, and first steps flooded them with emotion. Or perhaps my request interrupted an adult conversation. I'll never know, but something else, something bigger than me, was going on in the room. Rather than burdening the scout with complexities infinitely more profound than the scouting badge, my parents stooped to help. Without abandoning the self-centered pursuit of the badge, I nevertheless perceived a truth that dwarfed the weaving badge.

We all have weaving badges—things that are important to us. Over my shoulder, you peer as a reader, but my braid of a book is dwarfed by the enormity of your interior. Your reading is important, but your past and passions are more important.

Reading, as a writer explores his interior, is less messy than a reader exploring his or her interior. Your exploration is the important thing you've put to the side to read. As my cub scouting stirred unuttered truths within my parents, perhaps this book will stir unuttered truths in you. The braid was not, and the book is not, the most important thing in the room. Rather, the braid was used, and the book might be used to explore interiors. Your interior, even if unexplored and fearful, is far more important than this book.

Please consider using the unimportance of what you're holding as a nudge toward significance. You are important. Plumbing the depths of our individuality is important, though often avoided, work. As a divining stick senses underground water, I sensed significance on the kitchen floor. The book is to me what the badge was to me.

May this book be to you what the badge was to my parents.

May this book open a well of deeper meaning within you. My prayer is that you will stop and explore because prayer is all I can do. My selfish preoccupations kept me from asking my parents deeper questions. I needed the badge, and detours meant delays. I was too young to know I needed to stop to mark the moment's significance. You, however, are more perceptive than the self-centered elementary school child whose name I bear.

You have the capacity to recognize that whatever has drawn you to this reading has little to do with the reasons you need to be reading. I want you to read what I've written, but my desire is dwarfed by what's going on inside of you. Perhaps I'm still as selfish as I was on the kitchen floor. I wanted their help braiding, and they stooped. I want you to read, and you're still reading.

Read, not because what I have to say is important. Rather, read because the texts stir something within you that is beyond my initial grope at authorship.

The weaving badge was a win-win. I achieved a goal, and my parents discovered something that strengthened their lifelong commitments to each other. As a husband and father, I am more aware of how important the things that only your spouse can understand really are.

If you've been brought to plumb your interior, read no further. The most important work has been accomplished. If, however, my inward journey – much like my badge – complicates your life, let's continue. The badge and the entire scouting endeavor exposed an error in my thinking. I thought, as children often do, that I had most things figured out. Being stumped by the braid, however, meant I had to temporarily descend to the depths of the unenlightened chauffeur and laundress for answers. In their love, they answered the questions I asked them and released me again for important pursuits. I felt the weight of their intellect but had neither the interest nor the bandwidth to drink from their existential founts.

"Help me and leave me alone, unless I ask for help," kept me on a pedestal of self-assuredness.

Only in retrospect do I see that the pedestal was made of their shoulders.

Publication is exposing an error in my thinking. As my childhood was, so my adulthood is, occasionally deluded by the notion that I have things figured out. This book is a braiding badge of adulthood. My parents are not around anymore, so I am asking you for help. So far, you're helping. Selfishness clings to scouts and authors equally well. "Help me by reading my book," signals myopia, but "May reading this book help you," gives hope.

A long time ago, on the kitchen floor, I chose selfish ambition over depth. Thank you for giving me another chance.

## Chapter 1: A Drive To The Lake

Detroit is a car town.

My parents, Patricia and Alex Pickens Jr., were committed to Detroit. We worked in the city, worshiped in the city, and lived in the city. They were transplants from Maryland and Alabama.

Patricia McCallum earned degrees from Central State and Kent State Universities. She was trained as an educator because paths for Southern Black women were set in most people's minds. My mother had the courage to leave Baltimore, MD because she saw her older sister, Alice Fleshman Ledbetter Cooke, leave.

Pat stayed in Ohio after college because Baltimore, as she knew the city, could no longer contain her. She left Ohio because a jealous lover promised to kill her if she tried to leave him. Detroit provided a safe haven, steady work and another chance for love.

Alex came to Detroit in what Isabel Wilkerson[iv] called the Great Migration. Into her second marriage, his mother brought two sons before having two boys and a girl with Alex Pickens Sr. Alex matriculated through Detroit Public Schools before joining the US Air Force. Shortly after, an honorable discharge from Okinawa, Japan, he met Pat at a party.

Alex attended Wayne State University, married Pat, and became a private practicing obstetrician and gynecologist. I was the firstborn, but several pregnancies preceded me and Seth. Birth under an educator's wing meant early efforts to read, write, and count. We were enrolled in the Grosse Pointe Academy because my parents saw Detroit Public Schools as one of many options. Mom and Dad wanted us to see Whites up close and to know we could compete.

The Grosse Pointe Academy provided an excellent education, but suburban Detroit was a complicated place to go to school. I made friends and learned in beautifully manicured spaces, but I also absorbed adult complexities unsuited for children. Birthday parties in subdivisions with forty-year-old race-based housing covenants were fun, but they were not very funny.

Birthday parties are for children, but they're organized by adults. Pat and Alex were born in 1941 and knew when they were my age, they would have never been invited to Grosse Pointe Farms pool parties. Walking into suburban homes and staying to chat was, for them, about more than finding out what time to pick up Alex and Seth. Kevin G. Doyle[v] and Joe T. Darden[vi] have written of realities my parents understood; realities that belied the enthusiastic assurances that, "Alex is welcome anytime."

We pinned the tail on the donkey, but I was more fearful of being blindfolded than I should have been. What was important to me was not the most important thing in the suburban classrooms and living rooms I entered. While I was completing elementary and middle school, teachers and parents were digesting the Kerner Commission Report.

Published after the 1967 Detroit Riots, in which 43 people died, the report stated:

> Our nation is moving toward two societies, one Black, one White—separate and unequal. Reaction to last summer's disorders has quickened the movement and deepened the division. Discrimination and segregation have long permeated much of American life; they now threaten the future of every American."

This deepening racial division is not inevitable. The movement apart can be reversed. What the rioters appeared to be seeking was fuller participation in the social order and the material benefits enjoyed by the majority of American citizens. Rather than rejecting the American system,

> they were anxious to obtain a place for themselves in it.[vii]

I was born seven years after the 12th Street Riot, and my childhood was impacted by adults' memories of the flames. A complex history raised the stakes of my parents' responses to, "But why can't I? All of my classmates do."

"Why can't I go Up North? All of my classmates do." 'Up North' describes the Friday evening exodus and Sunday evening return for weekend recreation in parks, cabins, and boats. From Easter to Halloween, Michigan families spend weekends away but spend all week talking about where they've been. How can an elementary school child, listening to descriptions of a mysterious hinterland, do anything except ask to visit? My loving parents explained what they thought to be age appropriate. They knew, but waited to tell, more difficult truths about going 'Up North'.

> Idlewild is a small town in Yates Township, located just

east of Baldwin in southeast Lake County, a rural part of northwestern lower Michigan. During the first half of the 20th century, it was one of the few resorts in the country where African-Americans were allowed to vacation and purchase property, before discrimination was outlawed in 1964 through the Civil Rights Act of 1964.

Idlewild was founded in 1912. During this period, a small yet clearly distinguishable African American middle class – largely composed of professionals and small business owners – had been established in many urban centers, including several in the American Midwest. Despite having the financial means for leisure travel, racial segregation prevented them from recreational pursuits in most resort destinations in the region.[viii]

I was born ten years after the Civil Rights Act legally placed 'Up North' vacations within reach. Visiting wooded lakes, parks, and cabins, enjoyed for generations behind a segregated veil, can thwart a vacation's desired outcome. Getting away is supposed to relieve stress. Rather than leave me pining, my parents created alternative realities.

We drove to visit family members in Maryland and Alabama. Going 'Down South' became my ying to my classmates' 'Up North' yang. As their careers blossomed, my parents started a tradition of Caribbean vacations. Mass distraction worked so well that it became embarrassing to share which islands we visited. My classmates saw the same cabins, boats, and lakes each weekend and summer, but our parents were careful to provide unforgettable and diverse experiences. As we aged, we found out that peers spent vacations swatting mosquitoes or shivering in

Michigan lakes. Rather than divulge the corners of paradise we visited, all international vacations were dubbed as visits 'Down South'.

After eighth grade graduation, I needed something different. My parents allowed me to join family and friends at Martin Luther King Jr., Sr. High School. A bit too social and not serious enough academically, I was re-enrolled at the all-male University of Detroit Jesuit High School for the last three years of high school. Earning a driver's license was a rite of passage.

Detroit is a car town and driving 30-45 minutes to pick my brother up from the Grosse Pointe Academy was exactly what I wanted: freeway, tape deck and drive-thrus on demand. I was participating in a carpool of neighborhood families. We lived in or near the Boston-Edison District of Detroit and would ride together every morning and evening. While picking up my brother and neighbors, I was spotted by a Grosse Pointe police officer. Locking eyes with the officer would change my life forever.

Chapter 2: Uninformed Optimism

"Writing is something you do alone. It's a profession for introverts who want to tell you a story but don't want to make eye contact while doing it." ~ John Green

Silver spoons stir shame.

After editing the previous chapter, I was tempted to remove any mention of prosperity, travel, or notions I had ever dined sumptuously. Perhaps I will still cut out some of the 'God has been good' testimonials because, well, they're embarrassing. When so many are struggling, codifying an enchanted childhood seems boastful.

Recalling struggle, no matter how true, allows people to see themselves in you. If they suspect you've been through something like they have, they'll vote for you or pick you over another candidate. My childhood was supplied with two God-fearing parents,

Sunday brunches, and Easter suits. While I'm grateful, I will also never be a child again.

We've buried both parents. The house is gone. Any inheritance has landed in my stepmother's lap. Silver spoons are used for stirring and when we stir a solution, it changes.

Change is described by Brian Moran and Michael Lennington:

> It's helpful to understand the process we go through emotionally when faced with change, so we won't be derailed by it. Whenever we decide to make a change in our lives, we experience an emotional roller coaster. Psychologists Don Kelley and Daryl Conner describe this phenomenon in a paper called "The Emotional Cycle of Change." Kelley and Connor's emotional cycle of change (ECOC) includes five stages of emotional experience…" ~ The Twelve Week Year, pg. 69.

A police encounter changed my life. Locking eyes with an officer exposed me to the emotional cycle of change. Life took my silver spoon and stirred.

> The first stage of change is often exciting, as we imagine all of the benefits but have not yet experienced any of the costs. Our emotions are driven by our uninformed optimism…You see all of the benefits of the change and none of the downsides, so this stage is fun. You are brainstorming ideas and strategizing how you might create the new level of results you desire.
>
> Unfortunately, uninformed optimism doesn't last long. As you learn more about the reality of what it

> takes to change, positive emotions can quickly sour. ~ *The Twelve Week Year, pp 70-71.*

The previous chapter was my rendition of uninformed optimism. The remaining chapters are about three people's progression through the emotional cycle of change: yours, mine, and Elijah's. Emotional change occurs in all of our lives. With the Lord's help, I am inviting you to weave your life into a triple-braided cord with me and Elijah the Tishbite.

I Kings 17–II Kings 2 tell the story of Elijah the Tishbite. He does not share our benefit of anonymity. Rather, his life, warts and all, has been on display for over twenty-three hundred years. I picked Elijah because, after discovering *The Twelve Week Year*, his story tumbled into my life as if for the first time.

Clarity is a gift, and by God's grace, Elijah's story is clearer to me. Seeing his story helps me see my story.

Seeing two stories next to yours gives you the gift of clarity. If the book is all about me, what good is the book to you? An invitation, therefore, is extended to braid your life, within the confines of this book, into mine and Elijah's through the emotional cycle of change.

The cords we weave are the stories we tell. Elijah's is in black and white. This book will put my story in print as well, but you will benefit from anonymity. Wherever you're reading, you can use known stories to help you understand your story.

Change is coming.

The Easter suits are gone, and none of the shoes would fit if I could find them. I regularly visit the Caribbean, but only by gazing in my Jamaican wife's eyes. We gaze at each other over tea and take after-dinner walks. Inflation puts weekly Sunday brunches out of reach. There are splurges, but not like when I was little.

Things change, but sometimes we struggle. Adults sandwiched between dependent children and dependent parents know that things change. Conversations at high school reunions remind us that change is real. Parental deaths, sibling misunderstandings and empty nests bring change.

*The 12-Week Year* is a book about change.

Elijah's life is a story about struggle.

Reading both has led me to write about my struggle to change. Biblical authors lie in graves, and Moran / Lennington are authors I have yet to meet. God has used seemingly disconnected resources to help me deal with change. Your reading may help you deal with change.

At the end of each chapter, a set of reflection questions are your invitations to keep braiding your story into Elijah's and *The 12-Week Year*. If you are unfamiliar with the act of braiding, steps[ix] for braiding actual hair are:

1. Divide your hair into three sections. Use a comb to part your hair in two places to create three sections with even amounts of hair. One section is on the right side of your head, one in the middle, and one on the left side. Use your fingers to hold the sections separate from each other.
2. Cross the right section over the middle section. Keep the sections tight, so the finished braid won't come loose. Now the right section has become the middle section.
3. Cross the left section over the middle section. Cross the left section over the middle section. You've now completed the first segment of the braid. Keep holding the sections taut and apart from one another.
4. Continue crossing the right and left sections over the middle. Keep weaving the left section over the middle, then the right

section over the middle, always holding all of the sections taut and separate. Keep braiding the sections together until you run out of hair.
5. Secure the end with a hairband. Hold the braid in place by wrapping a hairband around the end, leaving a 1" unbraided tail to keep it secure.

My childhood was a fluffy pillow of uninformed optimism. Occasionally, my parents would say, "You know, some children don't go to Sunday school and eat peanut butter and jelly sandwiches everyday." They were trying to inform me about my optimism.

They wondered how their children were so far removed from their childhood experiences. Both were first-generation college graduates from southern states and able to recollect Jim Crow. Sometimes, before I tramped off in pressed slacks and polo shirts for private school matriculation, my mother would say, "If you walk with kings, never lose the common touch."

Nothing touches as commonly as fear.

## Chapter 3: Informed Pessimism

"There is no greater agony than bearing an untold story inside you." ~ Maya Angelou

The officer and I locked eyes, and he whipped a U-turn and started following me. After picking up the carpool, I headed home. The school children told me they wanted to stop for candy.

I pulled into a drugstore parking lot, sent the children to shop, and waited for their return. Once they were safely in the backseat, I started backing up to go home. Before I could get out of the parking space, an officer used his cruiser to block me. Trapped, I began to think of my parents.

When I received my driver's license, they sat me down and had what has since been dubbed 'The Talk'. German Lopez describes, ""The Talk" [as] the topic of a New York Times video from 2015, explaining how black parents have to prepare their sons for police encounters — out of fear, mainly, that such interactions can go horribly wrong, ending with their son dead."[x]

They talked, but I only listened long enough to get the keys. I was convinced that their race-based fears were erroneous in the enlightened age of the 1990s. Teenage bravado + parental concern = cold reasoning.

> "Cold cognition" is non-emotional information processing and reasoning. A person uses cold cognition to plan their schedule, consider the consequences of their actions, and evaluate different approaches to a problem. "Hot cognition" is decision-making in an emotionally charged situation that can result in an outcome with high risk or a high reward. Humans shift between these forms of cognition depending on their surrounding environment, physical and mental disposition[xi], and learn coping

mechanisms to high-stress events.[xii]

When they were having 'The Talk', I thought they were just talking. As the officer walked slowly toward the vehicle with his thumb on the holster, I was thankful for their counsel. I sat up straight, put my hands on the steering wheel at 10 and 2 o'clock, and told the children in the back seat to make no sudden movements. Rolling down the window, I found an agitated officer commanding, "Step out of the vehicle!" When I complied and inquired about the offense, he wordlessly spread me across the hood for a search.

After frisking, he demanded paperwork and went back to the cruiser without explanation. Eventually, I was told I fit a description of a recent bank robber. He pointed to the branch across the street, full of bankers watching the festivities. Returning the paperwork, he tipped his hat, climbed into the cruiser and drove away.

When he drove away, a sixteen-year-old and two seventh graders felt far from home. When I got home, I told my brother not to tell. He didn't, but the carpool members told their parents everything. Parents called parents, and I received another sit-down meeting. Assurances of love and support were mingled with questions and requests for clarification.

There was no blame, just concern. My mother and father saw my need, prayed for me, and filled me with warm food. They also put me back on the horse by keeping me in the carpool rotation. Back into the suburbs and past familiar landmarks I went, but I was different. Trauma changed my driving, attitude, and perspective.

I was OK but I wasn't OK.

Have you ever been OK but not OK?

Being OK but not OK is like wearing shiny shoes with a pebble inside. You look fine and may be the envy of your peers, but something is wrong. Muhammed Ali said, "It's not the hills we climb that get us. It's the pebbles in our shoes." We can fake it for a bit, but other people with pebbles in their shoes give short nods of recognition.

It takes one to know one.

I Kings 17:1-6 reintroduced me to someone who was OK but wasn't OK.

> Now Elijah the Tishbite, from Tishbe in Gilead, said to Ahab, "As the Lord, the God of Israel, lives, whom I serve, there will be neither dew nor rain in the next few years except at my word."
>
> Then the word of the Lord came to Elijah: "Leave here, turn eastward, and hide in the Kerith Ravine, east of the Jordan. You will drink from the brook, and I have directed the ravens to supply you with food there."
>
> So he did what the Lord had told him. He went to the Kerith Ravine, east of the Jordan,

> and stayed there. The ravens brought him bread and meat in the morning and bread and meat in the evening, and he drank from the brook.

Elijah's story began with a silver spoon.

Elijah walked with kings. During a famine, his needs were met. The Lord took care of Elijah the same way my parents took care of us. More miracles provided Elijah shelter, hospitality, and regular meals in a widow's home. While everyone around him starved, Elijah ate consistently, using a silver spoon of sorts.

Elijah's story began optimistically, but *The 12-Week Year* sobers.

> Unfortunately, uninformed optimism doesn't last long. As you learn more about the reality of what it takes to change, positive emotions can quickly sour. The second stage of change, informed pessimism, is characterized by

> a shift to a negative emotional state. At this point, the benefits don't seem as real, important, or immediate and the costs of the change are apparent. You start to question if the change is really worth the effort and begin to look for reasons to abandon the effort.[xiii]

Elijah' passed from uninformed optimism to informed pessimism. The traffic stop snatched me out of uninformed optimism and into informed pessimism. Has the silver spoon of steady-as-she-goes stirred pessimism in your life?

Elijah's bubble popped in the home of the widow the Lord miraculously fed.

> Sometime later, the son of the woman who owned the house became ill. He grew worse and worse and finally stopped breathing. She said to Elijah, "What do you have against me, man of God? Did you

come to remind me of my sin and kill my son?"

"Give me your son," Elijah replied. He took him from her arms, carried him to the upper room where he was staying, and laid him on his bed. Then he cried out to the Lord, "Lord my God, have you brought tragedy even on this widow I am staying with by causing her son to die?" Then he stretched himself out on the boy three times and cried out to the Lord, "Lord my God, let this boy's life return to him!"

The Lord heard Elijah's cry, and the boy's life returned to him, and he lived. Elijah picked up the child and carried him down from the room into the house. He gave him to his mother and said, "Look, your son is alive!"

Then the woman said to Elijah, "Now I know that you are a man of God and that the

> word of the Lord from your mouth is the truth."

The boy was flung into Elijah's arms by a desperate mother. Gone was the ease of earlier miracles. She watched Elijah go upstairs with the flattened juvenile chest cavity. She waited while the rafters creaked and were quiet; creaked and were quiet, creaked and were quiet. She marveled at her son's supernatural warmth and respiration.

Punctuation served as a tell for Elijah's shift from uninformed optimism to informed pessimism. It seems Elijah was stressed by the boy's choking. In place of his pattern of unquestioned reliance, the prophet questioned God. Alone in an upper room, the texts show Elijah unsure. The mother's accusation is ringing in his ears. A mix of prayer, action, and Elijah's first exclamation point preceded the boy's healing. Before the suffocation, Elijah was all commas and periods. A second exclamation point accompanied Elijah's offloading of his trauma into a mother's arms.

I read Elijah's use of a question mark, and an exclamation point, in the widow's house as a shift in mood and behavior. In my reading, the prophet seemed less composed.

Have you ever lost your composure?

The widow reaffirmed Elijah as a 'man of God.' You may have people who are willing to affirm you after you've been shaken. My parents dusted me off and threw me back into the carpool. A return to prophetic ministry, a driving rotation, or to business as usual can be helpful.
I Kings 17 persuades me that a near-death experience affected Elijah. A police encounter affected me. Reflective questions are your opportunity to consider shifts in your life.

Braiding Questions:

1. Have you ever experienced a shift from uninformed optimism to informed pessimism? If so, are you willing to write about your experience? Start with, "I

remember feeling a shift when…" and see where the sentence takes you.
2. Elijah cried out to God when the boy stopped breathing. When, if ever, have you cried out to God? Write the scenario and see where the writing takes you.
3. Elijah physically engaged the boy repeatedly. When has a breakthrough depended on prayer and your actual participation? Write what happened and remain open to where the writing takes you.

Chapter 4: Sensing Valley of Despair

"If you're going to have a story, have a big story, or none at all." ~ Joseph Campbell

My traffic stop flipped a light switch in my brain. My parents avoided going 'Up North' because of a history of segregation. Avoiding suburbs seemed just as wise. As they chose to create a 'work hard, play hard' narrative in the Caribbean, I chose to work and play in urban spaces. After high school, I picked big cities because they were full of Black people, and I understood the rules. Washington, DC, Baltimore, and Chicago served as undergraduate and graduate educational backdrops. I returned to Detroit to marry Naudia and start a family, avoiding the suburbs as much as possible.

When the children were old enough for school, we faced the same educational challenges my parents faced. Grosse Pointe Academy was chosen because Naudia loved the lakefront campus, and Catherine's grandparents were willing to help with tuition. Taking her to school, however, stirred memories of my time in Grosse Pointe Farms. Nothing serious, more like a faint queasiness. Because I failed to find language to explain, Naudia had no way of knowing why I didn't want to scout suburban neighborhoods for possible purchases.

I had unprocessed trauma from the traffic stop. I was afraid of filling the larger footprint that integration and career paths allowed. We could live wherever we wanted, but a twenty-year-old trauma restricted me. I was the same, but I was different.

Scripture paints a picture of Elijah being the same but being different.

> After a long time, in the third year, the word of the Lord came to Elijah: "Go and present yourself to Ahab, and I will send rain on the land." So, Elijah went to present himself to Ahab.

Now the famine was severe in Samaria, and Ahab had summoned Obadiah, his palace administrator. (Obadiah was a devout believer in the Lord. While Jezebel was killing off the Lord's prophets, Obadiah had taken a hundred prophets and hidden them in two caves, fifty in each, and had supplied them with food and water.) Ahab had said to Obadiah, "Go through the land to all the springs and valleys. Maybe we can find some grass to keep the horses and mules alive so we will not have to kill any of our animals." So they divided the land they were to cover, Ahab going in one direction and Obadiah in another.

As Obadiah was walking along, Elijah met him. Obadiah recognized him, bowed down to the ground, and said, "Is it really you, my lord Elijah?"

> "Yes," he replied. "Go tell your master, 'Elijah is here.'" ~ I Kings 18:1-8

Elijah was the same, but my reading showed his change.

I Kings 17 revealed Elijah initiating exchanges with King Ahab and the widow. He took the lead before the boy's suffocation. After the resuscitation, Elijah waited to be discovered instead of breaking the ice himself.

Extroversion set the tone in I Kings 17 but introversion seemed a theme in I Kings 18.

Extroversion and introversion are of particular interest to Susan Cain.

> When I started writing this book, the first thing I wanted to find out was precisely how researchers define introversion and extroversion. I knew that in 1921, the influential psychologist Carl Jung had published a bombshell of a

book, *Psychological Types,* popularizing the terms *introvert* and *extrovert* as the central building blocks of personality. Introverts are drawn to the inner world of thought and feeling, said Jung, extroverts to the external life of people and activities. Introverts focus on the meaning they make of the events swirling around them; extroverts plunge into the events themselves. Introverts recharge their batteries by being alone; extroverts need to recharge when they don't socialize enough. As a group, extroverts tend to be reward-seeking, but every human being has her own mix of approach and avoidance tendencies, and sometimes the combination differs depending on the situation. Indeed, many contemporary personality psychologists would say that threat vigilance is more characteristic of a trait known as "neuroticism" than introversion. The body's reward and threat systems also seem to work independently of each other, so that the same person can be generally sensitive, or insensitive, to both reward and threat. [xiv]

Elijah demonstrated extroverted behavior in I Kings 17. He appeared introverted at the beginning of I Kings 18. I can identify with Elijah's shifts.

Black Baptist church work runs on the fuel of extroversion. A mix of glad-handing, one-liners, and extemporaneous commentary is expected from the pulpit. While Susan Cain's "inner world of thought and feeling" is required for sermon preparation, teaching, and writing, a preacher does well to "plunge into the events" of Sunday mornings, potlucks, and social gatherings.

Finding a job as a Baptist pastor is kind of like winning a dice game. For sure, there are parts you control, but the whims of people are make-or-break realities. Extroversion is the name of the game; when it's time to say something, a preacher better have something to say.

Congregational leadership is not show business, but it is all business when the congregation shows up. In the 1990's and 2000s, congregational work in Detroit was synonymous with extroversion. Shined shoes, fresh haircuts, and tied ties had to gel with the ability to walk among the affluent and the afflicted.

My wife married the extrovert my parents groomed. My life was a I Kings 17 story.

Driving our daughter to the Grosse Pointe Academy turned the page of my life to I Kings 18.

In front of my wife and children, while working two jobs and attending night school, unprocessed fear began to gnaw.

Braiding Questions:

1. Do you need to be extroverted in some situations and introverted in others? If so, why? Write descriptions of each situation and reflect.
2. Write of a shift in your life, from uninformed optimism to informed pessimism.
3. Do you feel you are more naturally inclined to introversion or extroversion? Take Susan Cain's quiz[xv] and share the results with a trusted friend or family member.

Chapter 5: Entering Valley of Despair

"Story is a yearning meeting an obstacle." ~ Robert Olen Butler

> Rose bushes and other plants produce more buds than the plant can sustain. The plant has enough life and resources to free and nurture only so many buds to their full potential; it can't bring all of them to full bloom. In order for the bush to thrive, a certain number of buds have to go. The caretaker constantly examines the bush to see which buds are worthy of the plant's limited fuel and support and cuts the others away. He prunes them and takes them away, never to return. He ends their role in the life of the bush and puts an end to the bushes having to divert resources to them.

> In doing so, the gardener frees those needed resources so the plant can redirect them to the buds with the greatest potential to become mature roses. Those buds get the best that the bush has to offer, and they thrive and grow to fullness. But the rosebush could not do this without pruning. It is a necessity of life for rose bushes. Without the endings, you don't get the best roses.[xvi]
> ~ (*Necessary Endings*, page 16)

A church was looking for a pastor, and I was a preacher looking for an opportunity. The pastoral search was 'blind': our telephone and email exchanges never revealed the name or location of the church. Naudia and I bundled the children for the ninety-minute drive to the 'neutral pulpit'. With no home court advantage for the preacher and no premature exposure to the hiring church, the search committee took a good look.

We met next to a corn field, 'Up North' and sang 'Faith Of Our Fathers':

> Faith of our fathers, living still,
> In spite of dungeon, fire, and sword;
> Oh, how our hearts beat high with joy
> Whene'er we hear that glorious word.
> [Chorus]
> Faith of our fathers, holy faith,
> We will be true to thee till death!

A member of the search committee said, "Alex, when we drove here, we had a list of candidates but now we only have one: you."

Pastoring University Baptist Church was a high privilege and an enormous test. *The 12-Week Year* described my situation.

> I call the third stage the valley of despair. This is when most people give up. All of the pain of change is felt, and the benefits seem far away or less important. But there is a fast, easy way to end the discomfort: going back to the way you used to do things. After all, you rationalize that *it wasn't so bad before*. If you quit on change when you are in the valley of despair, you go back to the first stage, uninformed optimism, which is a whole lot more fun than being in the valley![xvii]

Yanked out of twenty years of urban living, I was flung into a village with the same socio-economic realities Grosse Pointe exhibited. My mother died the Wednesday before my first Sunday in the new job. My first impression was that the church was all White and the tiny town was full of police. I experienced the shock of a new community and a liminal fear of the police.

Election to a senior pastorate was exhilarating, but I was also thrown into a valley of despair.

> It is precisely at this stage—the valley of despair—that having a compelling vision is critical. Nearly all of us have had times in our lives when we wanted something so badly that we were willing to pay any price and overcome any hurdle to get it. Maybe it was your first car, maybe it was getting into that college you always dreamed of attending, maybe it was pursuing the person whom you wanted to marry, maybe it was your dream job—whatever it was, you wanted it so badly that you willingly paid the price of your own comfort to get it. Wanting passionately to reach your vision, combined with commitment and the tools and events of process control, is the way through the valley to the next stage of change.

I had a compelling vision, sparked by Patricia Ann McCallum Pickens. When I told her I wanted to preach, she was diplomatic.

> You may or may not be called to preach. We'll find out soon enough. When, however, they call because they need a preacher, there's a difference between your calling and your telephone ringing. Be careful.
>
> When you mount a pulpit, you might have a cold. Perhaps you narrowly escaped an automobile accident on your way to the church. Maybe you'll be negotiating heartbreak or loss. If something is amiss, there are two reasons not to tell the people.
>
> The first is that they don't care about your sickness, fright or burden.
>
> The second is that they braved the elements, sat in a pew, and

> offered their undivided attention because they were sick. Their lives have been turned upside down by random violence and misfortune. Their hearts are broken, and they've come for a word of hope. Your complaints work against your calling. If you can't lift them with the Word, get out of the pulpit and go find somebody who can.[xviii]

My mother died on a Wednesday, and my first day in the University Baptist pulpit was the following Sunday. Wise counselors advised postponement, and they were probably right. I was unwell. I was also unwilling to ignore the difficulties my mother described as tests for my preaching.

So, with a broken heart, I began learning a job that required behavior that was opposed to all I had been taught: out went the suits, and in came the polo shirts. Gone were the respectful titles I gave and expected. Rather, first names flowed freely from children to adults and from offspring to their parents. Calling the oldest member of the church by their first name had dire, perhaps permanent, consequences in Detroit, but 'Up North' casual familiarity was expected. I was excited to be a pastor, but three years of suburban living and a cross-cultural pastorate took a toll on my health.

A routine physical produced several follow up appointments. Primary care morphed into specialty care, and specialists made referrals. Tests, prods, and pokes revealed my symptoms were stress related. In a valley of despair, while my family watched me wither, Elijah the Tishbite began mentoring me.

Mentors never push their way toward influence in someone's life.[xix] Rather, a mentor earns the right to speak into the mentee's life. Quietly, for twenty-five years, Elijah walked alongside my Christianity in Old Testament obscurity. Before the loneliness of a pastorate, I had no ear to hear Elijah's lessons. After physicians and phlebotomists drained money, blood and sent me back to a difficult job, I saw myself in the suffocating boy.

Elijah had been waiting, my whole life, to help by sharing his story.

Braiding Questions:

1. Reread *The 12-Week Year* definition of a 'valley of despair'. Do you agree or disagree with the definition? Explain your answer in writing.
2. How have you passed from optimism to despair in your life? Explain your answer to a trusted friend or in a journal entry.
3. Can you think of an example of when you wanted to quit? Find a trusted listener and tell them what happened.

Chapter 6: Through the Valley of Despair

"There's always room for a story that can transport people to another place." ~ J.K. Rowling

> So Ahab sent word throughout all of Israel and assembled the prophets on Mount Carmel. Elijah went before the people and said, "How long will you waver between two opinions? If the Lord is God, follow him; but if Baal is God, follow him."
>
> But the people said nothing.
>
> Then Elijah said to them, "I am the only one of the Lord's prophets left, but Baal has four hundred and fifty prophets. Get two bulls for us. Let Baal's prophets choose one for themselves, and let them cut it into pieces and put it on the wood but not set fire to it. I will prepare the other bull and put it on the wood, but not set fire

to it. Then you call on the name of your god, and I will call on the name of the Lord. The god who answers by fire—he is God."

Then all the people said, "What you say is good."

Elijah said to the prophets of Baal, "Choose one of the bulls and prepare it first, since there are so many of you. Call on the name of your god, but do not light the fire." So they took the bull given to them and prepared it.

Then they called on the name of Baal from morning till noon. "Baal, answer us!" they shouted. But there was no response; no one answered. And they danced around the altar they had made.

At noon Elijah began to taunt them. "Shout louder!" he said. "Surely he is a god! Perhaps he is deep in thought, or busy, or traveling. Maybe he is sleeping and must be awakened." So they shouted louder and slashed themselves with swords and spears, as was their custom, until their blood flowed. Midday passed, and they continued their frantic prophesying until the time for the evening sacrifice. But there was no response, no one answered, no one paid attention.

Then Elijah said to all the people, "Come here to me." They came to him, and he repaired the altar of the Lord, which had been torn down. Elijah took twelve stones, one for each of the tribes descended from Jacob, to whom the word of the Lord had come, saying, "Your name shall be Israel." With the stones, he built an altar in the name of the Lord, and he dug a trench around it large enough to hold two seahs of seed. He arranged the wood, cut the bull into pieces, and laid it on the wood. Then he said to them, "Fill four large jars with water and pour it on the offering and on the wood."

"Do it again," he said, and they did it again.

"Do it a third time," he ordered, and they did it the third time. The water ran down around the altar and even filled the trench.

At the time of sacrifice, the prophet Elijah stepped forward and prayed: "Lord, the God of Abraham, Isaac, and Israel, let it be known today that you are God in Israel and that I am your servant and have done all these things at your command. Answer me, Lord, answer me, so these people will know that you, Lord, are God, and that you are turning their hearts back again."

> Then the fire of the Lord fell and burned up the sacrifice, the wood, the stones and the soil, and also licked up the water in the trench.
>
> When all the people saw this, they fell prostrate and cried, "The Lord—he is God! The Lord—he is God!" ~ I Kings 18:20-39

Elijah's encounter with the prophets was a high point in his ministry, but his victory came at a cost. I Kings 19 exposed Elijah's depth of despair so soon after a public victory on Mt. Carmel. God moved mightily, yet within a short time, Elijah was truly suffering.

God moved mightily at University Baptist Church. Situated across the street from fifty thousand students at Michigan State University, we had a cross-section of undergraduate, graduate, and doctoral students. Working professionals, local families, and retirees rounded out an intergenerational community of worshipers.

We initiated a mentoring program with Lansing Public Schools, baptized, married couples and buried loved ones. A three-bedroom, two-bath house was renovated and offered to student interns. Friends brought friends to church, and midweek gatherings grew. I began pursuing a doctoral degree, and our children made the transition much more quickly than we anticipated. Naudia's career progressed, and together we committed to retiring debt.

Election to University Baptist Church was a high point in ministry but our victories came at a cost. Sickness drove me to doctors and doctors sent me back home. Frightened by the severity of symptoms, I crawled into a closet and shut the door. Behind a veil of suits, shirts and ties - rendered irrelevant by my new job - I cried out to the Lord.

I began to pray, and the Lord revealed that my stress was related to fear. The socioeconomic status and race of my new neighbors mirrored those of families in Grosse Pointe Farms. When I saw the police, I felt like I was 16 years old again. I was sick because I was frightened. The Lord heard my cry.

> "I see you're afraid of the police, Alex."
>
> "Yup."
>
> "Do you fear Me?"
>
> "I fear you above all Lord. You are my light and my salvation. Whom shall I fear?"
>
> "If you believe Psalm 27, I want you to get off your knees, go to the police station, knock on the door and make some friends."

I avoided my assignment for weeks. Preaching and teaching are ineffective when the preacher and teacher are disobedient.

"Is this the Township Police Department?"

"Yes, how may I help you, sir?"

"I'm an urban Black male, living in-town, and I'm afraid of the police."

"Just one moment sir."

The cadet disappeared and returned with an officer. More questions and a background check led to the department inviting me to do a ride-along. I could ask the officer any question I wanted. Nothing was off-limits. I signed the waiver and crawled into a cruiser with an officer who was taller than my 6'1" frame and almost double my weight.

We began to patrol, and my nervousness was crippling. Near midnight, he set a speed trap in a rural area. I am the grandson of migrant workers from Alabama, and the last place I wanted to be was in the country, next to a White man with a gun. I feared a rope was next.

Between 1877 and 1950, four thousand African Americans were lynched.[xx] My grandfather, Alex Pickens Sr was born in 1906 and moved from Alabama with stories. As the Lord spoke to Elijah, so the Lord spoke to me. I was far from home, again, with a police officer because of what I heard in a prayer closet.

Fear is a stalking cat that pounces at inopportune moments. Prayer works against fear, and I began to pray for courage and protection. As I was silently praying, the officer began to share his pain.

He was a 17-year veteran with a wife and two children. His wife wanted what my mother and father wanted: to send their children to private school. To pay the tuition, he had to work overtime. Normally, rookies sit in the dark because the graveyard shift is the least preferred. He was working because he needed the money.

When he got home from the shift at 4 a.m., the children were asleep. When they got up to go to the fancy private school, he was asleep. He had worked several shifts in a row to get money for children he never saw. He hated it; he thought the public schools were fine, but his wife wanted private schools. So, he bit his tongue, pulled the shift, and suffered.

> "Why don't you find another job? You're missing their childhood."
>
> "I want another job. I don't like this one anymore. All I do is walk into people's nightmares over and over again. I can't fix what's wrong with people. I have high blood pressure, I'm overweight, and my doctors tell me stress is no good for me. But if I get out now, I won't get my pension."

His plan was to hold his breath for another 8 years and hope nothing happened to his marriage, his parenthood, his career, or his health; hope nothing happens on any of these emergency calls; hope that he was not ambushed; hope that he got to 25 years and the pension so that he could go get a job he really wanted.

> "Joe*, I'm here because I'm scared of the cops. I'm still working on that, but I don't need to be afraid of you. I need to be praying for you. What you're describing is horrible."
>
> "I'd love some prayer."
>
> "Okay let's get at it."
>
> "You mean right here?"
>
> "Yes, right here Joe. I'm a preacher from Detroit and I like to hold hands when I pray."
>
> After a long silence, Joe said, "Ok."

There was a shotgun between me and Joe. I slowly reached around the weapon, grabbed Joe's hand, and said, "Lord, this is my neighbor Joe; he's going through something, and he needs Your help. Please help him in Jesus's name." I put his hand down, and we formed a mutual understanding.

When I returned home, I was still afraid of officers, but I wasn't afraid of Officer Joe. I knew his story. Laying Joe's story next to Elijah's gave me courage.

Have you ever been afraid? A definition of courage that has helped me is 'fear in motion'. To be afraid and still is to be a target. To be in motion without fear is to exercise. Courage is fear in motion. A person in fearful motion makes a triple-braided cord that is not easily broken.

You are invited to complete your braiding questions.

*Name changed to protect an identity.

Braiding Questions:

1. How is your life similar to Elijah's? How is your life different?
2. Can you make a list of people you consider mentors?

3. Can you make a list of people in your life who need the benefit of your life experience? Make a list of the ways you can begin sharing what you know.

Chapter 7: Informed Optimism

"Do it again." ~ Elijah the Tishbite

A review of my journals reinforced the influence of a particular member of the University Baptist Church. I heard a testimony about God's use of a ride-along in the member's life during the same period of disobedience that led to my own ride-along. I asked the member to contribute to the book. At the time of publishing, the contributor was undecided about the use of the contributor's first and last name.

The agreement to write anything at all reinforces the lesson of the fourth stage of the emotional cycle of change. When I began writing, I was unsure if anyone would be willing to work with me. I started writing because I felt called to the work.

As I started writing before inviting this chapter's contributor to write, the contributor started riding along before inviting a congregation to ride. The Holy Spirit is at work, even in the fourth stage of the ECOC.

The fourth stage is informed optimism. At this stage, your likelihood of success is much higher. You are back in the positive emotional area of the cycle. The benefits of your actions are starting to bear fruit, and the costs of change are lessened because your new thoughts and actions are becoming more routine. The key at this stage is to not stop!

I am grateful this chapter's contributor endured an emotional cycle of change. Because of another believer's testimony, my life has forever changed.

_____
_____
_____

Anonymous Contribution:

Sin. Tragedy. Heartbreak. Consequences. A revolving cycle that is a reality of our fallen world, and a pattern we're all familiar with, some more intimately than others.

Sometimes, we're on the periphery of someone else's tragedy but sucked into the epicenter of the associated unfurling consequences. This was the case for me over several years, as I found myself in the middle of a complicated situation with a young man who had experienced deep pain and suffering. To make a very long story short, I endured a period of intense stalking and failed personal protective orders, which culminated in a felonious assault taking place on a college campus. In the aftermath, after victim impact statements, hearings, and sentencing, I tried to move on with my life as normal; however, it was anything but. Months after the "resolution" of the event, after wildly seeking anything (but the Holy One!) to numb the reality of my trauma, I found myself unable to get out of bed, deal with viral meningitis … or a mental breakdown. I had to withdraw from university and was barely able to care for myself. In the midst of clinical depression, PTSD, and OCD, I was desperate for peace … and purpose.

"Come to me all you who are weary and burdened, and I will give you rest," His Word called out to me. "Come along with me, my daughter," His Spirit whispered. At the end of my rope, I responded... and that act made all the difference. My journey to healing and wholeness was not a sprint to a magical finish line but, instead, the beginning of the best endurance run in which I've ever participated.

Looking to turn my pain into purpose, I eventually re-enrolled in university and changed my major to study criminal justice. If I had lived through such a disturbance in life and had the privilege of carrying this (what I have come to learn is an all-too-frequent reality) unique perspective of the Justice system, I may as well use it to help others. I initially thought this would entail supporting women coming out of domestic violence situations. This led me to pursue an internship with a law enforcement-adjacent, post-arrest response team that assisted survivors of domestic violence (DV). As part of the 40-hour long training, I also had to participate in a ride-along with a law enforcement officer (LEO) in order to learn more about the day-to-day situations a LEO is confronted with.

If I'm honest, I was scared out of my mind. My limited experience with LEOs included scary, deeply troubling situations … and I was about to spend several hours in the front seat of a cop car?! I really had no idea what to expect, but I was committed to my internship and knew I had to participate. I learned from the LEO about the real hardships of their job: the dangerous nature of the work, seeing the worst of the worst, and feeling frustrated when there are limited options to help people who have found their way—some by choice and some by consequences not of their choosing—into horrible situations. This LEO was sometimes on the periphery of other people's hardships and sometimes smack-dab in the center. Regardless, he was affected by all of it. To make another long story short, I was changed that day and motivated in a new way to assist a different group of victimized individuals—prostituted people. Marginalized people—women, mostly, but not always—that this LEO knew where to find on "the track" but was most days powerless to help. These were women that I saw in a new light, but I immediately recognized that I had been blissfully driving right by them for years.

This ride along, coupled with my successful internship and, a few years later, a burdensome call from the Father during an international missionary's talk on labor trafficking, led me to slightly switch gears again and become devoted to the fight against human trafficking. I shared my experience and everything I was learning with anyone who would listen, especially encouraging them to consider doing something scary and, likely, out of their comfort zone: participating in a ride-along! After several years of listening to His voice say, "Come along this way, my daughter," I pursued graduate education centered around human rights. In 2023, I celebrated ten years of meaningful, fulfilling work at an international anti-trafficking NGO.

Romans 8:28 rings so true for me. Out of sin comes redemption. Out of tragedy comes hope. Out of heartbreak, healing. In a fallen world, many times the consequences are sad or hard. Yet the consequences of hearing a call and responding with obedience to come along are life-changing and for good.

Chapter 8: Success

"I have stolen ideas from every book I have ever read." ~ Philip Pullman

> Success and fulfillment are the final stages of the emotional cycle of change (ECOC). At this final stage of change, the benefits of your new behaviors are fully experienced, and the costs of change are virtually gone. The actions, which at the beginning were difficult and uncomfortable, have now become routine. Every time you complete the cycle, you build not only your capacity but also your confidence. At this point, you can move on to the next change that you want to implement with greater assurance of success.[xxi]

A nine-year ministerial assignment at University Baptist Church (UBC) included the church's approbation of the chaplaincy. They watched me struggle, pray, obey, and ask, What's next?' Worshipers shared their testimonies. Musicians strengthened my heart, and the governing board added the officers to the missions budget.

In the first few years of the chaplaincy, I gave as much time as I could. As the years unfolded, I began wondering how I could minister more often among officers. Congregational demands were a priority, yet the cops tugged. Before discovering the emotional cycle of change, I was graced with the wisdom of the members of the UBC Leadership Council.

Each gray head was made available to their pastor. Elijah is a mentor, but Elijah can't hug me or brew a pot of tea. Real Christians walked with me in love as I made difficult decisions about my career. A church family celebrated our victories and sent me, with their blessing, to become a full-time police chaplain.

Some of the fruit of the emotional cycle of change is being shared with you in a collection of blog posts readers suggested for publication. Each story is linked to a fruit of the Spirit, mentioned in Galatians 5:22-23.

> *But the fruit of the Spirit is love, joy, peace, forbearance, kindness, goodness, faithfulness, gentleness, and self-control. Against such things, there is no law. ~ Gal 5:22–23*

May the fruit of the Holy Spirit bless and encourage you.

Fruit of Spirit

Love: A Downstairs Neighbor

Fried food wafted through the air. Some buildings smell like smoke, others like new carpet; this one smelled of food and fear. Neighbors peeked as Bert* knocked and announced, "Lansing Police Department..." An opened door revealed a tenant in white: matching headband, blouse, sweater, skirt and shoes. With halting English, she invited us in.

In the few seconds between her invitation and Bert's decision to stay in the hallway, the 911 caller opened his door. Through a translating roommate, he explained how the lady in white had been terrorizing the entire floor. Her calm stare and smirk confirmed that she was not afraid of the police.

Bert took the statement and finding no cause for arrest, distributed personal protective order (PPO) information. On our way back to the cruiser, one of the downstairs neighbors ushered us into her apartment. Holding up one finger she gestured, "Be quiet...wait a minute," while speaking into the cell phone and offering the Google translation to Bert.

Her screen told a story of abuse, assault, sexuality and rage surrounding the neighbor in white. Her apartment was below the lady in the white clothing, and she involuntarily heard and felt things through the ceiling. What she knew frightened her.

Speaking to the officer also frightened her. She resisted giving her name or filing a complaint because retaliation was probable. Seeing her torment, I whispered, "Fear hath torment..." (I John 4:18, KJV)

Google heard me and the translation flashed on her screen. When she read the translation, she began to nod and clap her hands. Worship followed as we connected around a shared faith. With tears, she let us know she believed in God, would avoid a public statement and just wanted authorities to know what was happening.

I let her know that Bert, and the Lansing Police Department, knew about what was going on. With more nodding, worship and translating she added, "...'ant taelam aydana" (Now you also know.)

"Yes, I know, and I will tell the One who knows all."

"shukraan jazilana. klu ma 'uridah hu 'an yuerifah 'ahad. (Thank you. That's all I want, is for someone to know.)"

Before leaving Bert and I read the rest of I John 4:18 over her, held hands and whispered a prayer of protection.

There is no fear in love; but perfect love casts out fear, because fear involves torment. But he who fears has not been made perfect in love. (I John 4:18)

She knew the words, but our visit reinforced their meaning. She was fearful when we entered the apartment, but Christ changed her fear into faith. Through prayer, the Word and her testimony she reported feeling better.

We were able to minister in her apartment because:

the Holy Spirit used a difficult situation for glorious ends;
the Lansing Police Department has a chaplaincy;
prayer partners cover the chaplaincy;

financial partners strengthen the work. Together we continue trusting Jesus for changed lives.

---

Prayer from the Apartment:

"Lord, we gather under a ceiling that is tormenting Your daughter. She has heard and felt things she wants to forget. We bring her to You because fear involves torment; she is tormented today.

Thank You for sending Bert to be what she needs in this moment. We thank You in advance for sending the Holy Spirit to occupy this apartment. We believe that there is no fear in love, but perfect love casts out fear. In the name of Jesus, we cast out the fear we found in this room.

We join our sister in trusting You to honor Your Word; to make her perfect in love by casting out fear, in the name of Jesus, amen.

_____
_____
_____

Joy: Story Time

Starting a new job is stressful.

Whether telecommuting or working onsite, jitters haunt. Mistakes bring learning, but stumbles are embarrassing. Getting lost, using wrong terms, missing subtleties and the weariness of acronyms/abbreviations can make anyone want to quit.

Endurance has tangled roots; visible grit comes from invisible sources. A family to feed, children to educate or parents to comfort timid workers. Peer pressure, debt or a lack of options spur some to action. Still others persevere because of a calling.

Responding to call is stressful: bone and marrow obey inaudible summons. The lieutenant was responsible for a room full of officers in their twenties. Some had expectant spouses or hungry children awaiting the end of the shift. Their youthful exuberance survived the police academy, interview process and the court of public opinion. Green, flexible shoots of public service swayed in the conference room.

The officer in charge was quick to call them young and green. They got lost, used wrong language and sometimes frustrated older officers. He also, however, made it his business to catch them doing things the right way. "Gotcha!" was a game he played for the shift's edification more than their humiliation. A job entrusting a Glock and rifle, with expectations they not be used, brings unique challenges. "LT" is an abbreviation for "lieutenant" and LT took every opportunity to encourage officers.

LT told stories.

Once, his grandmother cooked a goat head and set it before the family for Sunday dinner. His was a family that ate what was given; a working-class family; a public school attending, make the best of it family; a do your best and then some family; an if your grandmother is serving goat head you're going to eat goat head family. He smiled as he told the story in line up.

Line up is the part of the shift where all the officers gather. Special instructions, updates from the previous shift, things to remember and words of encouragement are sprinkled. Commanding officers establish the tone: some joke, others jeer. A recollection from his childhood let the entire shift into LT's inner room. In the room where his grandmother's steaming pot of goat head stew was offered, prayer preceded the meal. As his grandmother made space for prayer in the room she ran, so did her grandson make room for prayer in the room he ran.

"Chaplain, do you have a few words?"

The chaplain read I Timothy 4:12, "Don't let anyone look down on you because you are young, but set an example for the believers in speech, in conduct, in love, in faith and in purity." He went on to exhort the listeners.

> These words were written to a young man named Timothy. The writer knew what you've learned since starting this job: jitters haunt. Timothy suffered from a fear of failure. Messing up once can make each of us timid.
>
> Rather than cringe and hide, Timothy's mentor encouraged

him to set an example in speech and conduct. If anyone needs a word like Paul's to Timothy, it is law enforcement professionals. When you show up, your speech and conduct are recorded on dash cameras, body cameras and cell phones.

Internet traffic can leave officers feeling like Timothy: afraid to fail.

Each officer in the room needs what Timothy was prescribed: love, faith and purity.
All three are found in a personal relationship with Jesus Christ. As Timothy was called to serve in difficult situations, so are you. May love, faith and purity in speech / conduct be yours through the power of the Holy Spirit. Please know the food is sent by a team that is asking

the Lord to take you safely out and bring you safely home.

Via a team of prayer and financial partners, the chaplaincy provided cheeseburgers for LT's crew. In addition to sandwiches, LT gave the special instructions and updates from the previous shift. After a few problem-solving exchanges, each officer left for the road. With the room empty, LT shared the weight of responsibility he felt for each officer's life.

Quietly the chaplain listened while a seasoned officer told more stories; some for the very first time.

_____
_____
_____

Peace: A Simple Question

Imperfection is an inconvenience.

A graduate student's inconvenient question still echoes, "How do they respond to you when they're against you?" She perceived antipathy between white officers and black men and asked to interview me about the chaplaincy. Her question involuntarily brought me to the ministry's imperfection.

Law enforcement is a profession fraught with imperfections: innocent people go to jail; officers mistake identities; predators avoid prosecution. In a room full of cops with seniority, dozens of wrong decisions and injustices are undoubtedly represented. To be human is to be imperfect but thinking about imperfections, while ministering, is inconvenient.

Wondering how many wrongful incarcerations are represented in a gathering of twenty cops is unhelpful. God knows the number - just as God knows how many times I have stumbled in husbandry, parenthood and ministry - but thinking about the number saddens. Honest conversations with graduate students, are to the Lord what cattle prods are to ranchers.

A rancher calls the shots, not the cattle. When it's time to move, some beasts move sooner and some later, but they all move eventually. As on a ranch, so in the Kingdom. When the King says move, graduate students are sent with simple questions to remind reluctant believers Who is boss.

Q: How do they respond when they're against you?
A: It depends on the cop. Some are against God and want nothing to do

with chaplains. They are polite and may even say, "Good morning sir," but there is no interest in spiritual matters. Others are willing to engage in spiritual conversations, and even share their testimonies but are unwilling to engage in racial dialogue. Our conversations are in confidence but fear of saying the wrong thing is real.

There are also cops who think something is desperately wrong. They see peers making decisions based on skin color and tie prejudice to the Fall. We've had conversations about the Lord, race and scripture to explore solutions.

Q: How do you respond when they're against you?
A: I respond by looking beyond them, to Christ. Matthew 5:46-47 says, "If you love those who love you, what reward will you get? Are not even the tax collectors doing that? And if you

greet only your own people, what are you doing more than others? Do not even pagans do that? Be perfect therefore, as your heavenly Father is perfect." How cops treat me is less important than how I treat cops. On particularly difficult days, I remember that Jesus' last encounters with imperfect people in uniform was on a cross.

If I am taking up my cross and following Him daily, my doubts become lesser things. I may still be racially profiled, falsely identified or imprisoned. I look past difficult truths to see Him as Truth. Crucifixion was a Roman death, yet scripture shows the Lord loving and serving Roman soldiers before and after His death. Jesus helped Roman soldiers and I fix my eyes on Him while serving among cops.

(End of Interview)

An interview proved an inconvenient reminder of what it means to be a sheep under His rod.
Christ is using imperfect prayer and financial partners to send an imperfect chaplain among imperfect law enforcement professionals.

May His perfect will be done.

---
---
---

Patience: Ride Along Reflections

Chaplain Ed gave me books, advice and a bulletproof vest before he retired.

His books have been read and his vest worn but his advice proved most valuable. "Alex, if you're going to connect with cops, you have to ride." To "ride" means accompanying an officer on the road during a shift: in uniform, with the vest, applying book learning in the field. Officers with lowest seniority are often assigned ride-alongs with the chaplain. They're great teachers, open to conversation and curious about the chaplaincy. I am learning about shortcuts and situational awareness.

Shortcuts:
Each cruiser is equipped with GPS but officers just starting out are encouraged to learn street names and landmarks by memory. Learning how

to read a paper map is also encouraged because technology failures must not prevent arrival to a scene. If the GPS isn't working, an adequately trained officer can still find his or her way.

Riding with officers has opened the city to me in unexpected ways. Lansing, MI is split by a river into the North Side and South Side. Demographics, history and housing stock differ on either side of the river. Some streets are one way, some dead ends and some are shortcuts between neighborhoods. Ride alongs have also underlined the importance of situational awareness.

Situational Awareness:
Ride-alongs are often at high speed with lights and sirens. A city blurring past the window can be confusing, but cops maintain a sense of situational awareness. They can call out cardinal directions (north, south, east, west) on

the radio, under duress. Nighttime rides are especially disorienting.

I began riding on first shift (6 am - 4 pm) while our children were in school. The sergeant in charge of the chaplaincy said, "Thank you for riding, Alex, but we need you to spread the love to every shift." Rides expanded to second shift (3 pm - 1 am) and third shift (8:30 pm - 6:30 am) and I learned situational awareness. Day or night, it's important to know where we are and how to communicate a location to other people.

A ride along is an intrusion. Many cops patrol alone, their passenger seats double as desk space for snacks, paperwork and bags of equipment. By sitting in the passenger seat for the entire shift, I am intruding. Situational awareness of my disruptive presence has uncovered the short cut of listening.

Asking open-ended questions, and leaving space for a cop's thoughtful answers, can build a connection. During moments of silence, prayer can be a shortcut to situational awareness. The Holy Spirit reveals opportunities to serve.

Clearing debris, directing traffic, occupying children and holding a flashlight are little things the Lord reveals as opportunities to add value. Reading one of Ed's books, while cops are writing reports or making phone calls, allows silent accompaniment. Listening, busy work and coffee / donuts are paths that prepare hearts for the Good News of God's unconditional love. A ten-hour shift in the cruiser is an amazing mission field. Ed was right about the ride along.

I not only connect with cops, but the ride-along is also a short cut to situational awareness. Ed's books, advice and a vest continue equipping me to use the Gospel to serve first responders at the intersection of faith and public health.

_____
_____
_____

Kindness: A Brick, A Knife

A rookie cop found a sticker on his locker that read, "You've been visited by a member of the Ku Klux Klan."

He complained to supervisors and the sticker was removed. Outraged peers commiserated, decrying the injustice. Young cops, black and white, began dreaming of the changes they would make one day.

As they dreamed of change, 911 calls pulled them into nightmares: domestic violence, homicides, kidnappings, assaults, rapes. Thefts, stabbings, gunshots, suicides and car accidents pushed their dreams to the back burner. "Let's make a change," became "Let's make it home tonight." One of the young dreamers was injured.

Injured young dreamers were sent home until physicians clear them for service. His home was an hour away from work, allowing commuting time to think. At work, younger cops learned from experienced cops; rotating from one training officer to another. His injury changed his perspective. After a few shifts with a particular trainer, he felt familiar outrage. He knew his trainer was one of several who knew about the sticker. He began to understand why citizens despised the police. He knew his injury was tied to the change for which he and so many of his peers wanted to fight.

He was injured because a more experienced officer was heavy handed with citizens. Citizens' complaints and court appearances produced little change. Some community members were frustrated, and an ambush was set targeting anybody wearing blue.

It all happened so quickly after he received a call about a missing child. Remembering his own niece and nephew, he approached the house with compassion. Climbing the porch, caution chilled him, though he didn't know why. His knock on the door preceded the brick to his ear, the knife to his arm. He hunched, rolled, drew and fired.

Seven, maybe ten, seconds on a block patrolled by a sticker-placing peer, changed his life forever. News cameras and headlines emphasized the racial tension surrounding his injury. The ringing in his ear, possible nerve damage and post-traumatic stress disorder derailed his career.

Bills started stacking and his wife's belly started protruding. Officers who had placed, removed or ignored stickers, reached out with food, money and rides to pre-natal visits. They weren't perfect people but when he was down, they were family.

The ringing stopped, the baby was born and he returned to work. Night after night, close calls diminished his focus on fighting departmental injustice. "Let's just get home," became his mantra. He began to receive opportunities for promotion. The obdurate "way we do it here" blunted his hunger for righteousness.

He had hungry children and needed his job. The longer he stayed, the more cops retired. Sticker-placing cops retired; sticker-removing cops retired; cops unaware of stickers retired. Rookies began to ask him the same questions he used to ask. Before he knew it, seventy percent of the officers in the department had less experience than him. Less senior cops were hungry for righteousness and change. They saw strife between cops and the community and wanted to do something about it. Their idealism was tested when they rushed into nightmares far from home. They looked to him for leadership. "How do we do it around here?" they asked.

He thought about the sticker on his locker; thought about his zeal at the beginning; thought of the brick and the pain killers; thought about his gratitude for brothers and sisters in blue. He thought about the churches, families, schools and businesses that showed their appreciation. He thought about his first marriage, ruined by police work and the second he really wanted to work. He thought about the overdoses, the cars in the river, the sirens and wailing mothers; thought about the children and senior citizens.

"Work with what you have," he told the younger cops. "Take care of each other. Everyone goes home after the shift. You are the author of your career; it is what you make it. Wait for backup and remember your most important asset is between your ears.

"Think quickly, speak slowly and listen. Get help when you need it. This job can take your family and sanity. Keep them both. Bad things happen so learn how to cope. Exercise, get sleep and be a better version of yourself tomorrow than you were today. Keep learning. Shine your shoes. Be on time. Documentation matters. Make sure you..."

The radio beckoned him to the next emergency call. He hoped to finish telling them what he knew, but for now, he had to climb the next porch to knock. A child was reported missing.

_____
_____
_____

Goodness: A Promise & A Prayer

Police radio chatter can be disorienting. "Ten" codes drive covert conversations. Ten-four means "I heard what you said". Ten-eight, ten-two, ten-ninety-nine all mean something. I'm still learning, but equally disorienting can be the sound of my name coming over the radio.

A little after midnight, radio traffic requested a chaplain.

My cop asked what I wanted to do. I nodded.

"Ten-four, en route".

On the way, I felt a queasy curiosity. What could be going on at 1 a.m. to require a chaplain?

We arrived, rode the hospital elevator and found a family in mourning.

Security, cops, screaming, finger pointing, weeping, pacing, wailing and shock saturated the air. In an emergency, we default to our lowest level of training. I defaulted to scripture.

"Those who mourn will be comforted." (Matthew 5:4) Jesus promised, but there was no comfort in sight.

"Who's leading the family?" All eyes fell on BJ. "Can we talk?" Curiosity calmed people as BJ and I huddled.

"What happened?"

"Admitted this week...we were visiting MK regularly... a complicated surgery... now this."

The work of the Spirit is real. What I said doesn't matter as much as what the Lord did. A dozen family members were brought to see that MK needed their best that night. A police matter was distracting from the importance of the work of honoring their loved one. Anger was held next to their love.

Most gathered; a few walked away when I called for prayer. The willing held hands and bowed together. We asked God to keep a promise to comfort the mourning.

What could be going on to require a chaplain? I still don't really know; I walked into a situation that required the Word. They prepared to see the body. BJ consoled his family. Security slackened. We left.

"Those who mourn will be comforted."

Ten-four.

_____
_____
_____

Gentleness: Light Duty

Injuries abound among law enforcement professionals: ankles, shoulders, hands and knees; elbows, wrists, necks and backs. When an officer is injured, light duty is assigned.

Light duty is a noncontact sport: paperwork, websites, telephones and text messages; recovery, therapy, doctor's orders and email. On light duty, an officer still comes to work but has to watch peers do what circumstances momentarily prevent. Day after day, a light duty officer watches everyone disappear into the city while remaining at the station. Each person is different but the emotional toll for many is heavy.

Imagine the difference between an elementary school student doing an Easter egg hunt and watching one.

Discovering light duty added another layer to the chaplaincy because officers are inert, reflective and available.

When a 911 operator assigns an emergency to an officer, communication is facilitated with "10-codes". Dispatch understands the officer is on her way to the emergency when the assignment is accepted: "10-4". Upon arrival, the officer lets the 911 call center know she's arrived on scene: "I'm 10-2". Once on scene, the officer speaks to citizens more than the dispatcher but the dispatcher wants to know what's going on.

Imagine asking your peer to go into a scary basement. You're communicating at the top of the stairs and all the way down but when your friend turns the corner, communication stops. Peering into a potentially hazardous void is a head game: imaginations run wild. Dispatchers stand at the top of the stairs and officers descend basement steps.

At set intervals, operators check in because radio traffic slows once an officer begins interviewing victims, finding out who's telling the truth, collecting evidence, turning on the lights, siren, body camera and flashlight. As phlegmatically as possible, the operator asks, "What is your welfare?" Waiting for an answer rattles the veterans and rookies alike, as the entire department listens to for the answer.

Sometimes the answer is "10-2. Command staff, other officers and 911 operators understand the need to sound calm on the radio and the "10-2" is offered as placidly as the welfare inquiry.

Sometimes an answer is delayed and dispatch has to whisper into the basement again. This time the badge number or handle is added to the welfare check, "Ida 20, what is your welfare?" Dozens of people are listening to the radio traffic and all are aware the dispatcher has called into the dark basement a second time because there was no answer.

Preternaturally, the shift places meals, conversations and non-essential activities in abeyance because they are waiting for the "10-2". An eventual "10-2" exposes dozens of versions of feigned indifference; each an effort to communicate, "I wasn't scared and barely listen to the radio." In actuality, a conscious cop coils like a rattlesnake while waiting for the "10-2".

Readiness is required after delayed welfare checks because the response is sometimes, "I'm fighting, send two, units" or "Pursuing on foot near (cross streets named)". The officer on scene sounds like she is perched under a beach umbrella with a drink in hand but her heart rate may be in the mid-one hundreds. Dispatch acknowledges the call for help by very politely using another officer's handle to ask, "Adam 26, can you assist Ida 20?" Six or seven police cars have already started racing through the city with lights and sirens, at breakneck speeds, to help to Ida 20 but Adam 26 controls his breathing before purring "10-4". Dispatch may request another officer in the same way; a monotone response masking terror, "Am close, at (cross streets named)".

Often Ida 20 gets things under control and cooly croons, "I'm 10-2, you can disregard." Speedometers stop quivering and sirens stop howling but the deed is done. Everyone is amped, in motion and hypervigilant but uninitiated listeners to radio traffic would never know. Light duty officers have however been initiated.

They know a peer needs help, want to help but are forbidden from springing into action.

Light duty is fertile ground for the chaplaincy because the abovementioned can happen several times on a shift. After Ida 20 wraps up on scene, she lets dispatch know she's ready for the next call, "I'm 10-8" but everyone, including the light duty officers, rode the roller coaster. There is often little time to stop and say, "That felt terribly and I need a minute to get myself together." Like a conveyor belt, dispatch assigns the next emergency and the next. An injured officer can hear, and be tortured by, what is unsaid on the radio. When injury prevents coiling to anticipate assistance, talking about it helps. When chaplains find out someone is injured, we bring food or cold water to pass the time as we talk.

Whatever we bring is underwritten by a team of prayer and financial partners. Most of the work is listening rather than speaking. Few think of light duty officers while waiting for the "10-2" but if the chaplain is present, an injured constable knows he's not alone. Prayer works at a distance and is rarely refused by someone who would be racing into an emergency if health allowed.

Light duty stirs questions like, "Who am I if I can't do this job? My identity is wrapped into being a cop!" Sitting with people while they discover answers may take a few conversations over several weeks and when appropriate, an assurance of God's unconditional love is woven into our talks. Scripture provides the best answers I can offer.

I go into light duty praying because time alone allows things long suppressed to bubble to the surface.

An officer might be jovial one week and weeping the next; expectant on Monday and depressed on Thursday. Dozens of people are praying alongside the work and their focused petitions work among injured officers.

The Lord Jesus is using the chaplaincy to minister to light duty officers and we give Him glory.

_____
_____
_____

Faithfulness: A Voice In The Wilderness

"You again? What do you want?!"

"Hank*, someone called because they were worried about you."

"Worried about what? I was asleep and doing fine until you came along."

"They might have called to make sure you were alive."

"I'm alive and now I'm awake. Don't you have anything better to do?"

"Yes we do. Have a good morning Hank."

The officer explained that Hank's family was very supportive: out-of-state treatment, housing and unconditional love. Relatives may have wanted him off the street but Hank was clear about what he wanted: self-medication, sleeping on sidewalks, foraging. His choices allowed him to remember officers' faces and vice versa. Tommy* backed away from Hank's pile of blankets to take the next 911 call.

Hank was caustic in ushering us out of his open-air bedroom, but his poetic tone lodged in my imagination. A sing-song lilt powered his monologue. As we rode, I asked questions about Hank and Tommy readily shared what he knew. A few hours later, Hank was holding court, shirtless and barefoot, at a traffic light.

No sign or mendicant's stance accompanied his lecture. The strange brew of Tommy's knowledge, Hank's posture and our limited time between 911 calls amplified the Holy Spirit's, "Look and listen." We parked so Tommy could make sure Hank was not going to jump into traffic. I tried - without sounding like someone who believes he hears from God...when no one else in the truck seems to hear what God is saying - to say, "Tommy, may I get out, walk over to Hank and listen to his meandering, disjointed diatribe?"

"Sure chaplain."

Exiting, walking across the parking lot and crouching in the grass felt ridiculous. There was no plan but to obey a whispered "look and listen." How often do we approach someone standing at an intersection without looking? If we look, maybe we'll read the heartbreak scrawled on cardboard. If we listen to the heartbreak, we may be moved to alter plans and deviations can feel foolish. Budgets, plans and schedules seem smarter than compassionately listening and looking. Where are the coins and bills dropped in an outstretched hand really going? Sometimes it's easier to look away.

Hank looked at me.

"Can you repeat that last part? The traffic is loud and I missed it."

He sat up, exhaled - as geniuses exhale when enduring knaves - and asked, "What did you miss?"

"The part about radio waves and the red house."

His shoulders shrugged in a nonverbal, "You really are listening, aren't you?" He straightened his spine, a gesture saying, "finally...someone who really gets it." On cue, he repeated the previous word picture before pivoting to the next mind-bending image. Traffic continued to fly by and Tommy kept doing what he was supposed to be doing. For a little while, Hank had someone genuinely listening to his emphatic utterances. He was grateful, and so was I, for the unbroken minutes of our full and mutual attention.

> "He is a voice shouting in the wilderness, 'Prepare the way for the LORD's coming! Clear the road for him!'" ~ Mark 1:3

By the time we left for the next call, Hank had more bottles of water and bags of food than he could finish. He had cash for which he never asked. Drivers stopped, looked, listened and gave without solicitation. They gave compassionately at a red light while the chaplaincy gave the gift of undivided attention.

Hank felt heard because a team of prayer and financial partners sent a listener to ride with Tommy.

On patrol, Tommy and I spoke more about Hank, his family and the urban wilderness he calls home. Challenges remain. Tommy began to open up about some of his family's trials and triumphs. Later in the shift, when prayer was offered, he said yes. We bowed our heads together, thanked the Lord for safety on the shift and lifted our wives and children in prayer.

Together we were able to use the Gospel to serve human populations at the intersection of faith and public health.

*Name changed to maintain anonymity

_____
_____
_____

Self-Control: Go and Knock

The Saturday after George Floyd's death, the telephone rang. A friend's church was gathering for the first time since the COVID-19 quarantine and the pastor wanted me to speak. "You're a Christian, black and run with cops. We think you might have something to say."

I spoke of Peter having a friend who died in broad daylight in the presence of keepers of the peace. Peter spent weeks in fearful hiding because of his friend's public death at the hands of centurions. Seven years after his friend's death, the Lord told Peter to visit the home of a centurion. With doubts, he went.

George Floyd died in broad daylight in the presence of keepers of the peace. Protests and riots erupted because he died at the hands of police officers. He had a broad nose, brown skin, a short haircut and finished high school in 1992.

I finished high school in 1992, have a broad nose, brown skin and a short haircut. In 1990 I was traumatized by police officers, spent twenty-one years fearing police and suburban spaces until the Lord told me, "Fear Me, not cops. Go down to that police station, knock on the door and make some friends."

The Lord spoke to Peter.

> "Simon, three men are looking for you. So get up and go downstairs. Do not hesitate to go with them, for I have sent them." Peter went down and said to the men, "I'm the one you're looking for. Why have you come?" The men replied, "We have come from Cornelius the centurion. He is a righteous and God-fearing man, who is

respected by all the Jewish people. A holy angel told him to ask you to come to his house so that he could hear what you have to say." ~ Acts 10:19-22

A centurion was a keeper of the peace with eighty to one hundred people in his command. The city in which the Spirit spoke to Peter was within sixty miles of the site where his friend died publicly. Cornelius' city was also within sixty miles of Peter's friend's grave. Centurions commanding hundreds of people were unique; there was a limited number within a sixty-mile radius.

Cornelius the centurion probably knew the centurion who was present when Peter's friend was crucified. Peter probably saw Roman centurions regularly and may have been able to identify the one who gave the order to remove Jesus from the cross. Cornelius might have finished school in the same year, had the same haircut and Roman facial features as the centurion with orders to seal the tomb. If two centurions were in a room full of civilians, they would have involuntarily nodded at one another because they lived a reality few understood.

Kimberly D. Manning, MD describes the centurions' nod in a Journal of the American Medical Association article.

> In my experience, the black-on-black nod of acknowledgment is usually given in situations where only a few other black people are sprinkled through an environment together. For example—when I enter a PTA meeting at my sons' school (where the attendees are predominantly non-black), without fail the handful of ethnically similar parents in the room automatically exchange nods with me.[xxii]

Centurions would have nodded, the way black people nod, the way cops nod.

I would nod at Peter but only the Lord knows if he would nod back. As centurions gave him pause, so cops gave me pause. As the Lord spoke to Peter, so did the Lord speak to me. As Peter walked toward his fears, so did I walk toward my fears. Peter went with the men, entered Cornelius's house and shared the Gospel of Jesus Christ. I knocked on a precinct door in 2012, did my first ride along and unexpectedly shared Christ with a cop.

In 2014, I applied as a part-time chaplain and in 2018 became full-time. I continue to serve, with George Floyd's video playing in my mind, for the same reason Peter served through flashbacks of Jesus' torture: Christ compels.

Jesus' sinless frame was battered for my sins, cops' sins, Peter's sins and centurions' sins. Peter was thankful enough for Jesus' death to walk into the house of a man whose rank was unattainable without the spilling of blood. I am thankful enough for Jesus' death to turn my broad-nosed, dark-skinned, middle-aged frame toward the precinct. I minister among officers because Christ ministered among centurions.

> When he had entered Capernaum, a centurion came forward to him, appealing to him, "Lord, my servant is lying paralyzed at home, suffering terribly." And he said to him, "I will come and heal him." But the centurion replied, "Lord, I am not worthy to have you come under my roof, but only say the word, and my servant will be healed. For I too am a man

under authority, with soldiers under me. And I say to one, 'Go,' and he goes, and to another, 'Come,' and he comes, and to my servant, 'Do this,' and he does it." When Jesus heard this, he marveled and said to those who followed him, "Truly, I tell you, with no one in Israel have I found such faith. ~ Matthew 8: 5-10

I minister among officers because Peter minister among centurions.

So, Peter opened his mouth and said: "Truly I understand that God shows no partiality, but in every nation anyone who fears him and does what is right is acceptable to him. As for the word that he sent to Israel, preaching good news of peace through Jesus Christ (he is Lord of all), you yourselves know what happened throughout all

Judea, beginning from Galilee after the baptism that John proclaimed: how God anointed Jesus of Nazareth with the Holy Spirit and with power. He went about doing good and healing all who were oppressed by the devil, for God was with him. And we are witnesses of all that he did both in the country of the Jews and in Jerusalem. They put him to death by hanging him on a tree, but God raised him on the third day and made him to appear, not to all the people but to us who had been chosen by God as witnesses, who ate and drank with him after he rose from the dead. And he commanded us to preach to the people and to testify that he is the one appointed by God to be judge of the living and the dead. To him all the prophets bear witness that everyone who

> believes in him receives forgiveness of sins through his name." ~ Acts 10: 34-43

George and Mike and Philando call from the grave. Some hear and protest, others hear and riot. Some hear and legislate; others hear and beef up training.

I hear a call to remember what to do when people die in broad daylight among peace officers. Peter hid, heard from the Lord and obeyed with everything he had. I hid from cops for twenty-one years, heard from the Lord and am taking the next obedient step.

Honesty reveals my doubt that a chaplaincy is effective. My assignment is, however, worth more than my doubts. I'm going to do what He says and, in this season, He's saying, "Go down there, knock on the door and make some friends."

I read Peter and remember George's head bobbing publicly. I read of Jesus and recall his head bobbing publicly.

Then I go, knock and share Christ, trusting He is the Friend who sticks closer than a brother.

---

One For The Road: A Happy Ending

She was seven years old, thumbing a ride.

"Where are you going?"

"Away from here."

"Why are you leaving?"

"My grandmother is a demon...sister too."

"How do you know they're demons?"

"Because they say stupid things and are unreasonable."

Her unreasonable grandmother waved from the house. A quick huddle with grandma confirmed that she was keeping four other children in the house while the mothers were away. A morning of generational conflict spurred hitchhiking. We discovered the traveler dressed in a snow suit and mittens.

"Do you have any food?"

"No."

"Where are you going to sleep tonight?"

"I don't know."

"Do you feel safe in your grandmother's home? Is there anything the officer in the driver's seat needs to know?"

If a child is being hurt, chaplains are mandatory reporters. We discovered her after leaving a 911 dispute elsewhere on her grandmother's block. Sometimes demons play roles in the police being called. Greed, anger, grudges and cruelty impact granddaughters and grandmothers; sisters and parents alike. Finding out if a child is in the clutches of hellish imps is part of the work. Officers' body cameras run during encounters with the community, no matter how benign. Bantering with an elementary schooler could turn into something more serious. Turning my back to her grandmother, we spoke in lower tones. I asked again and the cyclopic eye on his chest watched closely.

"I feel safe."

"Is leaving a warm house, without food as the sun is setting, stupid and unreasonable?"

"Maybe."

"Are you a demon?"

"No."

"Is your grandmother a demon?"

"No."

"It's cold outside. If we give you some stickers, will you put the bags back in the house?"

"Will you turn on the lights and siren too?"

"Deal."

Off she went, dutifully keeping her end of the bargain. Back on the curb, the officer made her day. She sat in the front seat, collected her stickers and saw all the gadgets. A peek in the backseat and quick Q&A did the trick.

"I want to be an officer," she whispered before bounding onto the porch and into her grandmother's arms. Watching their reconciling embrace was a welcome switch; not all of the conversations that night had happy endings.

We talked about her on the way to the next call. He had only demonstrated the cruiser to one other child and was glad to get another chance. Listening to his relief reminded me that his profession exposes him to demonic situations.

"Do you believe in demons, officer?"

"I do."

"Can you tell me more about what you believe?"

With ease, he began to open up about his childhood, marriage and faith. Theological discussions were interspersed between the 911 calls. We met the hitchhiking deal maker before sunset but spoke of faith, struggle and healing all night. He had questions and scripture was offered in response, "Come unto me, all who are weary and burdened, and I will give you rest." (Matt 11:28)

Deep into the ten-hour shift, the Lord sparked opportunities. His hero sandwich was purchased because generous partners give to the chaplaincy. He heard scripture because the Bible is central to the chaplaincy. A listening ear was available to an officer because of the prayer team's intercession. In the wee hours, he said "Something has been bothering me, chaplain. Can we talk about it?"

"Absolutely. What's going on?"

In hushed tones, he confided.

A trained and listening ear was available during his shift because a team of ministry partners sent me with regular generous prayer and financial support. To facilitate his introspection, I asked open ended follow up questions until the end of the shift. When offered prayer, he paused before responding, "Absolutely."

In the parking lot of the Lansing Police Department, we held hands and bowed our heads. Together we took our weariness to Jesus and trusted Him to give us rest.

Addendum

And though one may be overpowered, two can resist. Moreover, a cord of three strands is not quickly broken. ~ Ecclesiastes 4:12

Mentoring is, also, a consideration of three strands.

A mentor, or experienced advisor, is trusted by one less experienced. Wherever someone is unsure, and someone else knows the feeling of being unsure, a mentoring relationship is possible.

Careers are influenced by mentors, as entry level employees will attest. If you know someone, your chances of being someone in the organization increase. While important, mentors are not all-powerful. They still find themselves unsure.

This is a book about mentoring. One strand of the book is the mentor's, and a second strand is mine, but the third strand is yours.

Dolph Smith, a Memphis-based mixed media artist, says, "My work is unfinished without interpreters. If I make something and it sits there, my work is unfinished. My work is finished when people take the art into their hearts. When you find meaning in what I do, my work is finished."[xxiii]

A book is finished when a reader finds meaning and I have found meaning in the life of an unsure individual. I have no claim on his victories and no responsibility for his defeats, yet my life is tied to my mentor.

I have connected to him by reading his story and pray you will connect to him through my story. You, my mentor and I make a cord of three strands, not easily broken.

Mentoring is, also, a consideration of three strands.


Alex Pickens III
09Jun23
Memphis, TN

Acknowledgements

Adults have a line at their heels.

Free throw lines, service lines and cafeteria lines consider what is ahead, but adulthood is impossible to consider without looking back.

My most important childhood decision was trusting Jesus. I heard the Name above all names at my mother's knee. Pat Pickens told me she was the number one woman in my life, until a wife took her place. I believed her. Alex Pickens Jr. told me wedding rings are heavy but strength-building. I believed him.

My most important adult decision has been marrying Naudia. She is the third strand of a me-and-Jesus cord. There are few things to which I affix personal pronouns, but she is my wife and Catherine and Christian are our children.

My family has watched the unsure progression of my career, including this book project, with curiosity.

Thank you for loving me while I burned logs and read Tolstoy.

Big thanks to the Chiefs of Police who've allowed me to minister at the Lansing Police Department. Mike Yankowski, Darryl Green and Ellery Sosebee had the ability to sweep chaplains away with a pen stroke. Each has provided access, support and keys to closely guarded doors. I am grateful.

Gratitude abounds for Ed Owens. Dave Leisman and Frank Weller agreed that Ed was the chaplaincy's lead horse. Thank you for your books and bulletproof vest. Serving as a chaplain with Father Bob Irish, Clyde Carnegie, Rosalinda Hernandez, Drew Filkins and Damon Milton has been an honor. Lori Hagle, Barb Houghteling, Ruth Grant, Hazel Bethea and Cherice Fleming have diligently kept chaplains informed.

Our liaison officers - Ryan Cressman, Shawn McNamara and Ryan Kellom - have facilitated trusted access to hundreds of police officers. Darren

Southworth's response to, "What am I supposed to be doing as a chaplain?" has been golden. "Chaplain, it is what you make it."

A heterogeneous mix of White, Black, Latin X, adoptees, immigrants, LBGTQI, single, married, divorced and 'it's complicated' people have eaten all the cheeseburgers. I thank the Lord for the local, regional, state and federal professionals, sweating and freezing in Old Harry Hill High School.

Gas to and fro has been provided by Reliant Mission. Big thanks to Keva Ambre and the June 2018 training cohort for support-raising coaching. Tom Mauriello inked the book deal and Dave Meldrum-Green tells amazing IRS war stories. Much love to every Reliant-affiliated prayer and financial partner including 242 Church, American Baptist Churches of MI, Kingdom Life, Shekhinah, Capital City Vineyard, Chilson Hills, First Baptist DeWitt, Mason Community, Mount Hope, Christ's Kingdom Builders, Pilgrim Rest Baptist, Pilgrim United Methodist, Praise Baptist, Lily Baptist,

Aurelius Baptist, Bethel Baptist, Charlotte AG, Christian Celebration Center, Church Alive, City Life Lansing, Columbia Road Baptist, Crossroads Lansing, Detroit Church of Christ, Element, Epicenter of Worship, Faith Fellowship Bible, First Baptist Wyandotte, Galilee Baptist, Greater Rose of Sharon, Hope In the Hills, Imagine This, Impact Orlando, New Hope Community, New Prospect Baptist, Northpointe Community, Olivet Baptist, Riverview, South Main Baptist, St. Luke Lutheran, Sunfield United Brethren, Second Baptist of Detroit, Unitarian Universalists of Greater Lansing, Voice of Power Deliverance, West Angeles COGIC, Zion Hill Baptist.

Authorship has been aided by the 2016 Dean of Harvard Chapel's pearl, "To write well we have to read well." I was improbably whisked to Cambridge, MA because William Shiell called my name.

Seeking Jesus, with Jessie Still and the House Of Prayer East Lansing, is something everyone should do at least once. Keturah and Coye Bouyer, Christy and Gabriel Castillo, Amy and Jack Lumanog, Tayana and Sean Holland and Karen & John Bell are confidants and friends.

The Holy Spirit flows through Pilgrim Rest Baptist Church. For each of our pastors - Walter Gibson, Maurice Scruggs, Dwight McQuirter, and Ed Rockett - thanksgiving overflows. Walter Stoudamire, Evangelist Matthews, and Johnny Mendenhall are able mentors.

Jim Bontrager and the International Conference of Police Chaplains have provided training and camaraderie. Manning Brown, Denny Geisenhaver, and Keoki Awai break bread, laugh and pray with me. An alternate universe has been opened by the Billy Graham Rapid Response Team and Samaritan's Purse.

Mark Kring, Rich Bruce, and the New Hope Haslett Church family introduced us to Samaritan's Purse and size 14 Keens. Steady encouragement to write has come from Rich, Guy

Dorsainville, Judy Ellis, Bill Brewer, Charissa Grace, Semira Washington, Sucre Woodley, Isis Pickens, Steven Turner, Torrey and Shannon Oliver, Marvin Williams, and Wallace Johnson Jr.

Thanks to Roy Mireles and Tony Henry for letting me sweep the floors and take out the trash. Eloise Johnson and Revaune Edmonson have been answers to prayer. Big up to the Tending Vision blog readers who have cheered, scolded, and commented.

Sabarras George, Bob Diamond, and the Michigan Athletic Club staff let me scream at the bottom of the pool. Steve Shadrach, Scott Morton, and Ellis Goldstein were the first voices I heard say, "It's OK to preach and expect to be able to feed your family."

Thanks to Denise and Kevin Turman, Michael Williams, Brian Johnson, Adam Metzger, Dan Miller, Steve Malson, Paul Langford, Dallas Flippin, Ken Beesley, Jim Stolt, John Harris, Zach Bartels, Nicole and Ben Brandt, Jeff Chan, Dustin Edwards, Jasmine

Brown, Jamil Scott, and Charle Pickens for calling out to the dry bones.

Seth Watson Pickens is my blood brother, born for a time of adversity. Thank you for our Tuesday and Thursday flow.

# Bibliography

Boy Scouts of America. (2023, September 15). *www.scouting.org*. Retrieved from www.scouting.org: https://www.scouting.org/page/4/?s=required+adventures+chart+for+ranks#cl-group-2

Burns, J. (2019). *Doing Life With Your Adult Children.* Grand Rapids: Zondervan.

Cain, S. (2013). *Quiet: The Power of Introverts In A World That Can't Stop Talking.* New York: Crown Publishing Group.

Cain, S. (2023, September 15). *https://susancain.net*. Retrieved from https://susancain.net: https://susancain.net/quiet-quiz/

Cloud, H. (2011). *Necessary Endings: The Employees, Businesses and Relationships That All Of Us Have To Give Up In Order To Move Forward.* New York: HarperCollins Publishers.

Darden, J. T., & Thomas, R. W. (2013). *Detroit: Race Riots,*

*Racial Conflicts, and Efforts to Bridge the Racial Divide.* East Lansing, MI: Michigan State University Press.

Doyle, K. G. (2004). *Arc of Justice: A Saga of Race, Civil Rights and Murder in the Jazz Age.* New York: Henry Holt and Company.

Equal Justice Initiative. (2023, September 15). *www.eji.org*. Retrieved from www.eji.org: https://eji.org/reports/lynching-in-america/

History.com. (2023, September 15). *1967 Detroit Riots*. Retrieved from History.com: https://www.history.com/topics/1960s/1967-detroit-riots

Lopez, G. (2023, September 15). *www.vox.com*. Retrieved from www.vox.com: https://www.vox.com/2016/8/8/12401792/police-black-parents-the-talk

Millstein, S. G., & Halpern-Felsher, B. L. (2002). Perceptions of Risk and Vulnerability. *Journal of Adolescent Health*, 412-413.

Moran, B., & Lennington, M. (2013). *The 12 Week Year: Get More Done In 12 Weeks Than Others Do in 12 Months.* Hoboken, NJ: John Wiley & Sons, Inc.

Niang, N. A. (2023, September 15). *www.wikihow.com.* Retrieved from www.wikihow.com: https://www.wikihow.com/Braid

Olson, R. E. (2023, June 09). *www.patheos.com.* Retrieved from www.patheos.com: https://www.patheos.com/blogs/rogereolson/2013/01/did-karl-barth-really-say-jesus-loves-me-this-i-know/

Pickens, P. M. (2002, August 19). Mrs. (A. P. III, Interviewer)

Smith, D. (n.d.). Wadell, Withers and Smith: A Requiem For King. *Wadell, Withers and Smith: A Requiem For King.* National Civil Rights Museum, Memphis, TN.

Walker, L. (2023, September 15). *Idlewild Black Resort.* Retrieved from www.purehistory.org:

https://purehistory.org/idlewild-black-resort-michigan/

Wilkerson, I. (2010). *The Warmth of Other Suns: The Epic Story of America's Great Migration.* New York: Vintage Press, Random House Inc.

Zimmer-Gembeck, M. J., & Skinner, E. A. (2010). Adolescents coping with stress: development and diversity. *School Nurse News*, 23-28.

Zondervan. (2011). *New International Version Bible.* Grand Rapids, MI: HarperCollins Publishers.

About The Author

Alex Pickens III, of Detroit, MI, attended Howard University and studied international business. He also served as an Assistant in the Andrew Rankin Memorial Chapel before deploying as a missionary to Zimbabwe.

As a Peace Corps Volunteer, he was appointed the Director of Development for Junior Achievement International (Cote d'Ivoire) before earning a Master of Health Science in Finance and Management at The Johns Hopkins Bloomberg School of Public Health.

While at Hopkins, Alex proposed to Naudia Bryan. They are married and have two children. Catherine Ruby was born nine months before her father earned a Master of Divinity from McCormick Theological Seminary. Christian Ethan was born five months before his mother earned a Doctor of Medicine from Michigan State University.

Alex served as the Assistant to the Pastor at Second Baptist Church of Detroit and as the Senior Pastor of University Baptist Church of East Lansing, MI. He has a Doctor of Ministry from Northern Baptist Theological Seminary.

More information on his work is available at www.tendingvision.com.

Endnotes

i https://www.mindtools.com/apjsz96/kelley-and-conners-emotional-cycle-of-change

ii https://www.patheos.com/blogs/rogereolson/2013/01/did-karl-barth-really-say-jesus-loves-me-this-i-know/

iii https://www.scouting.org/wp-content/uploads/2018/08/Required-Adventures-Chart-for-Ranks.pdf

iv Wilkerson, Isabel: *The Warmth of Other Suns: The Epic Story of America's Great Migration.* 2010 published by Vintage Press

v Doyle, Kevin G: *Arc of Justice: A Saga of Race, Civil Rights, and Murder in the Jazz Age.* 2004 published by Henry Holt & Col

vi Darden, Joe T: *Detroit: Race Riots, Racial Conflicts, and Efforts to Bridge the Racial Divide.* 2013 published by Michigan State University Press

vii https://www.history.com/topics/1960s/1967-detroit-riots

viii https://purehistory.org/idlewild-black-resort-michigan/

ix https://www.wikihow.com/Braid

x https://www.vox.com/2016/8/8/12401792/police-black-parents-the-talk

xi 1 Millstein, S., & Halpern-Felsher, B. (2002). Perceptions of Risk and Vulnerability. Journal of Adolescent Health, 31(1), 10–27. doi: 10.1016/s1054-139x(02)00412-3.

xii 2 Zimmer-Gembeck, M., & Skinner, E. (2010). Adolescents coping with stress: Development and diversity. School Nurse News. 27. 23-8.

xiii Moran, page 71

xiv Cain, Susan. *Quiet: The Power of Introverts In A World That Can't Stop Talking*; by Crown Publishing Group in 2013 pp 171

xv https://susancain.net/quiet-quiz/

xvi Cloud, Henry: *Necessary Endings*, Harper Business, 2011

xvii Moran, pg. 71

xviii Patricia Pickens, circa 2002

xix Jim Burns. *Doing Life With Your Adult Children*. Zondervan, 2019, (11-minute mark of audio book)

xx https://eji.org/reports/lynching-in-america/

xxi Brian Moran, pg. 72

xxii

https://jamanetwork.com/journals/jama/issue/323/17

xxiii
https://www.askart.com/artist/artist/10050194/artist.aspx?alert=info#

Made in the USA
Monee, IL
27 September 2023